Roberto Clemente

Dona and William Rice

Consultant

Timothy Rasinski, Ph.D.
Kent State University

Publishing Credits

Dona Herweck Rice, *Editor-in-Chief*

Robin Erickson, *Production Director*

Lee Aucoin, *Creative Director*

Conni Medina, M.A.Ed., *Editorial Director*

Jamey Acosta, *Editor*

Heidi Kellenberger, *Editor*

Lexa Hoang, *Designer*

Leslie Palmer, *Designer*

Stephanie Reid, *Photo Editor*

Rachelle Cracchiolo, M.S.Ed., *Publisher*

Based on writing from *TIME For Kids*.

TIME For Kids and the *TIME For Kids* logo are registered trademarks of TIME Inc. Used under license.

Teacher Created Materials

5301 Oceanus Drive
Huntington Beach, CA 92649-1030
http://www.tcmpub.com

ISBN 978-1-4333-3683-6

© 2012 Teacher Created Materials, Inc.
Reprinted 2013

Table of Contents

The Pride of Puerto Rico

On August 18, 1934, something wonderful happened for Melchor (mel-CHOR) and Luisa Clemente. They had their fifth child, Roberto Clemente Walker, in the town of Carolina, Puerto Rico. Little did they know that one day their beautiful son would be known as the Pride of Puerto Rico.

Carolina, Puerto Rico

Nicaragua

Commonwealth of Puerto Rico

Nestled between the Caribbean Sea and the Atlantic Ocean, you will find a beautiful tropical paradise. It is the island of Puerto Rico. Puerto Rico is officially called the *Commonwealth of Puerto Rico*. In Spanish, the language spoken by most Puerto Ricans, it is called the *Estado Libre Asociado de Puerto Rico*. Puerto Rico is under the protection and leadership of the United States of America. Some people think that Puerto Rico may one day be the 51st state of the United States.

Latino Names

It is common for **Latino** children to be given their mother's **maiden name** following their own last name. That is why Roberto was also named Walker, his mother's maiden name, although his family name was Clemente.

Years ago, the **fertile** ground of Puerto Rico was dotted with sugar and coffee plantations. Many Puerto Ricans worked on the **plantations** or at the mills that made the sugar and coffee. Roberto's father was one of those workers.

A good and proud man in his mid-fifties, Melchor was a **foreman** at a Puerto Rican sugarcane mill. His wife, Luisa, did the laundry for the owner of the mill. Melchor and Luisa also ran a small grocery store.

the central mountains of Puerto Rico

coffee plant

Business in Puerto Rico

At the time of Roberto's birth, farming was the most common business in Puerto Rico. In the 1950s, industry replaced farming as the leading business. Tourism also became very important, with more than five million tourists visiting the island every year.

Nothing but Love

Young Roberto grew up with nothing but love in his home. As an adult, he said, "I never heard any hate in my house. Not for anybody."

Roberto's parents taught him to be a good person. They taught him to treat himself and others with respect and dignity, and they taught him the importance of hard work.

A Lesson Remembered

When Roberto grew up, he ran baseball clinics for children in Puerto Rico. In the clinics, he taught children the importance of hard work, respect, and being a good citizen. He never forgot the lessons of his childhood, and he wanted to be sure those lessons were shared and continued with others.

The Clemente family was also very generous. When poor children came to their home, Luisa fed them a good meal. Roberto learned that people who have been blessed with good fortune should share what they have with those less fortunate. This was a lesson that Roberto would always remember.

As Roberto grew, he worked very hard to make a difference in the world for himself and others. Once, he helped a group of children raise money to build a fence around their school for protection. Another time, he saved a person from a burning car!

Roberto started working when he was nine years old in order to save money to buy a bicycle.

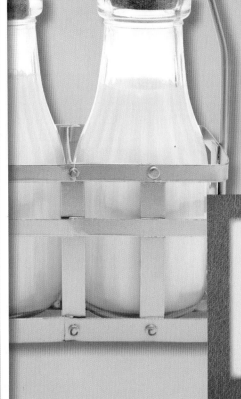

Milk Bottles

Years ago, milk was delivered to people's houses. When they finished the milk, they left the bottles outside for the milkman to take away.

Roberto got up early each morning to deliver milk for a penny a day. He saved his pennies for three years in order to buy a bicycle. When Roberto wanted to do something, he worked hard until the job was done.

Young Roberto dreamed of becoming a professional baseball player.

It's a good thing Roberto was such a hard worker. The ability to make something happen by working hard became even more important as he grew. That is because Roberto had a big dream. He dreamed of being a **professional** baseball player. Roberto said, "I am convinced that God wanted me to be a baseball player. I was born to play baseball."

Although he did not have much money for baseball **equipment**, Roberto still practiced his baseball skills. He repeatedly hit bottle caps with a broomstick. He threw tennis balls against a wall, catching them as they bounced back to him. He did whatever he could to become the best baseball player he could be.

Living the Dream

Roberto believed in his dream, so he worked hard to make it happen. He never stopped believing he would become a great baseball player.

A Dream Come True

All of Roberto's hard work paid off. While still in high school, he played professional baseball for the Santurce Crabbers in Puerto Rico. Then, in 1954, the Brooklyn Dodgers **drafted** him to play with their **farm club**. Best of all, in 1955, the Pittsburgh Pirates of the United States drafted Roberto to play on their major league team! He became the Pirates' right fielder—one of the best to ever play the game.

Roberto began playing professional baseball when he was still a teenager.

Bob Clemente

When Roberto first began playing in the United States, he was listed on the **roster** as *Bob Clemente*. His team thought his real name sounded too foreign, and they didn't want to use it.

Roberto made his debut with the Pirates in the major leagues on April 17, 1955.

Paving the Way

When Roberto started playing in the major leagues in the United States, it had only been a few years since someone other than a white person was allowed to play. Roberto was not the first Latino or black person to play in the major leagues, but he was the first black Latino to make a big difference in the game. No wonder he was known as the *Pride of Puerto Rico*!

What an Arm!

It is almost guaranteed that when a runner is on third base and the batter hits a single, the third-base runner will come home safely for a run. But Roberto's throwing arm was so good that he once threw out a player trying to score from third base on a single. People are still amazed by that play.

Roberto became known for his powerful swing, fast running, and amazing plays on the field. Many of the best pitchers of the time knew how hard it was to strike out Roberto. Roberto was so fast that his hat or helmet often flew off when he was running! Best of all for the fans, Roberto was almost an **acrobat** on the field. He covered very large areas of grass, running long distances to catch fly balls that many other outfielders could not catch in time.

Then, when he caught and threw the ball, the runner had to watch out! Most of the time, Roberto's powerful arm threw the ball to the base for the out long before the runner knew it was coming. There were not many runners who would try to take extra bases when Roberto was on the field.

Gotcha!

Roberto had such a strong arm when fielding that he led the **National League** in outfield assists during five of his professional seasons. An outfield assist is when an outfielder throws the ball to a base in time to make an out. Players of the time usually didn't try to take extra bases or take any chances when Roberto was on the field. Even so, he often got them out when they normally would have been safe.

Although Roberto was always a good player, his first big season came in 1960 when he led his team to a **World Series** win. The next year was big, too. Roberto was the National League batting champion.

Of course, playing baseball wasn't Roberto's only joy in life. On November 14, 1964, he married Vera Cristina Zabala. They had three sons, all born in Puerto Rico: Roberto Jr., Luis Roberto, and Roberto Enrique.

Roberto sits with his parents, his wife, and his children.

Pride of the Pirates

The night of the big 1960 World Series win, Roberto's teammates were together having a party. But Roberto knew the Pirates owed a lot to the fans who had supported them all season. Instead of going to the party, he wanted to walk the streets of Pittsburgh to thank the fans in person.

Making a Difference

Roberto is now considered one of the greats of baseball. Even so, he remembered the lessons he had learned as a child. He knew it was important to make a difference in the world, and it was important to help others.

Whenever younger Latino players joined the league, Roberto would do his best to give them a hand. He helped them to be the best players they could be. He helped so much that in 1966, his Latino teammate, Matty Alou, beat out Roberto for the batting championship!

brothers Matty and Felipe Alou of the San Francisco Giants

Being the Best You Can Be

Roberto always worked to be the best he could be. He was known for his loving nature and intelligence. Besides being an excellent baseball player, he wrote poetry, played the organ, made ceramics, and even studied **chiropractic** medicine!

Roberto once said, "If you have an opportunity to make things better, and you don't do that, you are wasting your time on this Earth."

portrait of Pittsburgh Pirates Roberto Clemente (second from left) and other baseball stars at the 1965 All-Star Game

Ballplayer and Humanitarian

Roberto's friend and teammate, Manny Sanguillen, said, "Roberto Clemente played the game of baseball with great passion. That passion could only be matched by his unrelenting commitment to make a difference in the lives of the less fortunate and those in need. People saw Roberto as a great ballplayer and **humanitarian**. He was also a great father, husband, teammate, and friend."

Roberto also looked around the world of baseball and saw many things that were unfair. While Roberto was one of the best players, he was never asked by any company to **endorse** its products in commercials or advertisements. Only white players were asked to do that. Roberto spoke out against this treatment. He knew that it was wrong and had to be changed.

He also thought that Latino baseball players were not treated as well as other players. For example, Roberto was troubled with neck and backaches, but people often doubted that his pains were real. But, when famous white players complained of the same things, no one ever doubted them.

It wasn't just in baseball that Roberto spoke out against inequality and made a difference. He also developed a friendship with Dr. Martin Luther King Jr. and worked with him to bring about equal treatment for all people. He joined many causes to help the poor and mistreated. Because he had good fortune, he knew it was his job to help bring good fortune to others.

Dr. Martin Luther King Jr. with other civil rights protestors during the March on Washington, August 28, 1963

While Roberto was working to make a difference in the world, he also continued making a difference on the baseball field. In 1971, his team won the World Series again. This time, Roberto was named the Most Valuable Player (MVP).

But an even bigger win for Roberto came late in his career. After several years of breaking down prejudice against Latino players, Roberto believed things were changing. He said, "My greatest satisfaction comes from helping to erase the old opinion about Latin Americans and blacks." This was among Roberto's proudest achievements.

One of the highlights of Roberto's career came in 1971 when he hit a home run in the last game of the World Series.

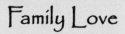

Family Love

After winning Most Valuable Player, Roberto was asked how he felt. He responded with a message for his parents. He said, "On the greatest day of my life, I ask for your blessing."

Last Great Achievement in Baseball

On September 30, 1972, the last day of the regular baseball season, Roberto earned his 3,000th career hit. He was the 11th player in major league history to earn 3,000 hits in a career. That was the last hit Roberto would ever make.

Roberto Clemente and the Mets' Willie Mays after Clemente's 3,000th hit. Mays and Clemente are both members of the 3,000 hit club.

Gone Too Soon

Roberto lived his life ready to help others and to make a better world. When a terrible earthquake struck the country of Nicaragua in 1972, Roberto knew he wanted to do something. The people of Puerto Rico were trying to send **relief** supplies to the people of Nicaragua, but there were challenges getting the supplies there. So, Roberto decided to deliver the shipments himself. On December 31, 1972, his plane took off from San Juan, Puerto Rico. Shortly after takeoff, it crashed into the ocean. Roberto and the others on board were killed.

In Puerto Rico, Pittsburgh, and around the world, people **mourned** the loss of not only a great baseball player, but also a great man.

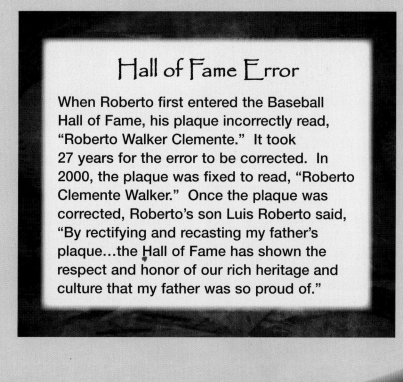

Hall of Fame Error

When Roberto first entered the Baseball Hall of Fame, his plaque incorrectly read, "Roberto Walker Clemente." It took 27 years for the error to be corrected. In 2000, the plaque was fixed to read, "Roberto Clemente Walker." Once the plaque was corrected, Roberto's son Luis Roberto said, "By rectifying and recasting my father's plaque...the Hall of Fame has shown the respect and honor of our rich heritage and culture that my father was so proud of."

Throughout his long career, Roberto earned many awards and honors. He was such a great player and person that more awards came even after he died. The time line on the next page shows some highlights of Roberto's amazing career.

Roberto Alomar speaks to students at the Roberto Clemente Sports City in Puerto Rico.

Roberto Clemente Sports City

Late in his life, Roberto opened a sports city for the children of Puerto Rico to build their athletic skills and prevent drug abuse. Today, the Roberto Clemente Sports City is a nonprofit organization that continues the work he began.

Time Line

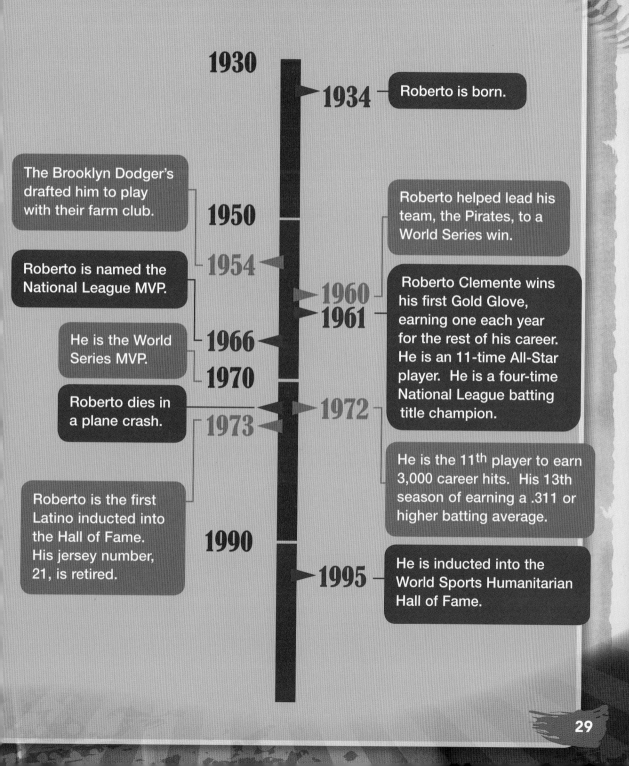

1930

1934 — Roberto is born.

The Brooklyn Dodger's drafted him to play with their farm club.

Roberto helped lead his team, the Pirates, to a World Series win.

1950

1954

Roberto is named the National League MVP.

1960

1961

Roberto Clemente wins his first Gold Glove, earning one each year for the rest of his career. He is an 11-time All-Star player. He is a four-time National League batting title champion.

He is the World Series MVP.

1966

1970

Roberto dies in a plane crash.

1972

1973

He is the 11th player to earn 3,000 career hits. His 13th season of earning a .311 or higher batting average.

Roberto is the first Latino inducted into the Hall of Fame. His jersey number, 21, is retired.

1990

1995 — He is inducted into the World Sports Humanitarian Hall of Fame.

Glossary

acrobat—a gymnast; a person able to move his or her body in amazing ways

chiropractic—a type of therapy that uses the body to heal itself and stay healthy

drafted—chose as a player for the major leagues

endorse—to approve or support a product in exchange for money

equipment—tools used to play a sport

farm club—a baseball team made up of players who are next in line to be pulled up into the major leagues

fertile—rich in everything needed for things to grow

foreman—the boss who manages a group of workers, usually in a factory, mill, or some other large business

humanitarian—a person who works for the health and happiness of other people

Latino—a person of Hispanic, usually Latin American, descent, usually living in the United States

maiden name—a woman's last name before she is married

mourned—took time to be sad about someone's death

National League—one of two leagues in Major League Baseball in the United States

plantations—large farms on which crops are grown

professional—a job for which a person is paid

relief—assistance in the form of supplies such as clothes, blankets, medicine, and food

roster—a list of people on a team

World Series—the top championship in major league baseball, played between the National League and American League champions

Index

About the Authors

Dona Herweck Rice grew up in Anaheim, California, and graduated from the University of Southern California with a degree in English and from the University of California at Berkeley with a credential for teaching. She has been a teacher in preschool through tenth grade, a researcher, a librarian, and a theater director, and is now an editor, a poet, a writer of teacher materials, and a writer of books for children. She is married with two sons and lives in Southern California.

William Rice grew up in Pomona, California, and graduated from Idaho State University with a degree in geology. He works at a California state agency that strives to protect the quality of surface and ground water resources. Protecting and preserving the environment is important to him. He is married with two children and lives in Southern California.